WORLDVIEW GUIDE

PILGRIM'S PROGRESS

Douglas Wilson

canonpress
Moscow, Idaho

Published by Canon Press
P.O. Box 8729, Moscow, Idaho 83843
800.488.2034 | www.canonpress.com

Douglas Wilson, *Worldview Guide for Pilgrim's Progress*
Copyright ©2019 by Douglas Wilson.
Cited page numbers come from the Canon Classics edition of the book (2017),
www.canonpress.com/books/canon-classics.

Cover design by James Engerbretson
Cover illustration by Forrest Dickison
Interior design by Valerie Anne Bost and James Engerbretson

Printed in the United States of America.

All Scripture quotations taken from King James Version.

Library of Congress Cataloging-in-Publication Data
Wilson, Douglas, 1953- author.
Pilgrim's progress worldview guide / Douglas Wilson.
Moscow, Idaho : Canon Press, [2019]
LCCN 2019011345 | ISBN 1591282497 (paperback : alk. paper)
LCSH: Bunyan, John, 1628-1688. Pilgrim's progress.
Classification: LCC PR3330.A9 W55 2019 | DDC 828/.407--dc23
LC record available at https://lccn.loc.gov/2019011345

A free end-of-book test and answer key are available for download at
www.canonpress.com/ClassicsQuizzes

19 20 21 22 23 24   9 8 7 6 5 4 3 2 1

CONTENTS

INTRODUCTION

The Pilgrim's Progress is a classic of classics. If we exclude sacred texts (the Bible, the Koran, etc.), liturgical texts (*Book of Common Prayer*), and political books that Chairman Mao might take a dim view of your family not owning (political propaganda), *The Pilgrim's Progress* is arguably the best-selling book of all time. It has never been out of print, and has been translated into over 200 languages. If you have not read it, you cannot be said to be educated in Western letters, and if you did not read it *appreciatively*, we might still have our doubts.

THE WORLD AROUND

A little over a decade before the publication of *The Pilgrim's Progress*, London was wracked by the Great Plague, the last outbreak of the Bubonic Plague in England (1665–1666). About a quarter of London's population died in that epidemic, meaning about 100,000 people lost their lives. 1666 was the same year that Bunyan's autobiography, *Grace Abounding*, was printed. The plague was topped off by the Great Fire of London, which destroyed much of the city center—although it did help with the plague by destroying rats along with houses. Given these judgments of "biblical" proportions, it is not hard to see why Bunyan's portrayal of the City of Destruction in 1678 did seem somewhat realistic. It was an apocalyptic vision, to be sure, but it came shortly after an apocalyptic time.

Charles II was king in 1678, and would remain so until his death in 1685. He was succeeded by James II, who reigned both briefly and poorly (the adverbs are related), and then William and Mary came to the throne in the Glorious Revolution of 1688—the year of Bunyan's death.

Across the water to the east, a woman from Venice became the first woman to receive a university doctorate. Her name was Elena Cornaro Piscopia. 1678 was the year that the first ship was built in America, a ship named *Griffon*, and it was built by Robert LaSalle. In hindsight, there were not a lot of significant events happening around the rest of the world, but the excitement in England made up for it.

ABOUT THE AUTHOR

John Bunyan was born in 1628, and died almost 60 years later in 1688. At the age of sixteen, he joined the Parliamentary Army and served in the English Civil War under Cromwell for about three years. After his stint in the army, he returned to his native Bedford, and took up the trade of tinker, which he had learned from his father. He married a pious young woman (we do not know her name, but an educated guess suggests Mary) and a short time after became intensely interested in religious matters. Although the Bunyans were very poor—according to Bunyan they did not have "so much household stuff as a dish or a spoon betwixt us both"—his wife brought two books into the marriage that would influence Bunyan greatly.[1] They were *The Plaine Man's Path-way to Heaven* by Arthur Dent, and *The Practice of Pietie*, by Lewis Bayly. After Mary died, leaving John with four children (Mary,

---

1. *Grace Abounding to the Chief of Sinners*, section 15.

Elizabeth, John and Thomas), John married again. His second wife was named Elizabeth, and John's imprisonment occurred shortly after his second marriage.

After Cromwell's Interregnum, when Charles II was restored to the throne, religious liberty for Puritans was greatly curtailed. This had a dramatic impact on Bunyan's life—he would spend twelve years in jail for his refusal to discontinue preaching. The issue was not "preaching" actually, but rather licensure. He was a nonconformist, and this meant he did not believe he needed to be licensed by the state in order to preach. During his time in prison, he wrote his spiritual autobiography *Grace Abounding*, and a good part of his most famous work, *The Pilgrim's Progress*.

Today the Church of England holds a Lesser Festival in his honor, and Westminster Abbey has a stained glass window doing the same, both of which John Bunyan would have thought to be pretty funny.

WHAT OTHER NOTABLES SAID

"May it please your Majesty, could I possess the tinker's ability for preaching, I would willingly relinquish all my learning."

~ John Owen, to King Charles II

"The greater part of it is enthralling narrative or genuinely dramatic dialogue. Bunyan stands with Malory and Trollope as a master of perfect naturalness in the mimesis of ordinary conversation."

~ C.S. Lewis[2]

"Anyone who is honestly trying to be a Christian will soon find his intelligence being sharpened: one of the reasons why it needs no special education to be a Christian is that

---

2. C. S. Lewis, *Selected Literary Essays*, ed. Walter Hooper, First Edition (New York: HarperOne, 2013), 198.

Christianity is an education itself. That is why an unedu-
cated believer like Bunyan was able to write a book that
has astonished the whole world."

~ C.S. Lewis[3]

"Have you never admired that portrait from the hand of
old John Bunyan?—a grave person with eyes lifted up to
heaven, the best of books in his hand, the law of truth
written on his lips, the world behind his back, standing as
if he pleaded with men, and a crown of gold hanging over
his head. Who gave that minister so blessed a manner,
and such goodly matter? Whence came his skill? Did he
acquire it in the college? Did he learn it in the seminary?
Ah, no. He learned it of the God of Jacob; he learned it of
the Holy Ghost; for the Holy Ghost is the great counsel-
lor who teaches us how to advocate his cause aright."

~ Charles Spurgeon[4]

"Next to the Bible, the book I value most is John Bunyan's
Pilgrim's Progress. I believe I have read it through at least
a hundred times. It is a volume of which I never seem to
tire; and the secret of its freshness is that it is so largely
compiled from the Scriptures."

~ Charles Spurgeon[5]

3. C. S. Lewis, *Mere Christianity* (New York: HarperOne, 2001), 78.
4. Charles Spurgeon, *Sermons of the Rev. C.H. Spurgeon* (New York:
Sheldon, Blakeman, and Company, 1858), 71.
5. Ibid., 253.

SETTING, CHARACTERS, AND PLOT SUMMARY

The narrator dreams of his protagonist, a man named Christian, who flees from his hometown, the City of Destruction, in order to make his way to his final home, the Celestial City.

Christian's pilgrimage wends its torturous way between the two cities, but the great transition on the way is found at his conversion—he comes to the place of the cross, and that is where the great burden of his sins rolls off his back.

The road between the two cities is marked by many places that typify the experience of many Christians—the Slough of Despond, Vanity Fair, Doubting Castle, the Valley of Humiliation, the Delectable Mountains, along with others. About each it may be said that this is the kind of place where this kind of thing happens.

This road is also a place where Christian encounters many individuals who represent the kind of people we meet in this life. His first sincere companion along the way is Faithful. After Faithful is martyred in Vanity Fair, Hopeful replaces him as Christian's companion. Less helpful among those encountered are Mr. Worldly Wiseman, Talkative, Pliable, the Flatterer, and Atheist. As with the places, it is easy to tell what each man does.

WORLDVIEW ANALYSIS

The book is not a suspense, although there is (mysteriously) plenty of suspense in it. It is an allegory related in the circumstances of a dream—a common enough device—and the allegory is about as straightforward as it is possible to get. The City of Destruction is on one end, and the Celestial City on the other. The protagonist is named Christian, and so *that* is cleared up. We don't have to wonder about the character of any individuals we meet—we don't need to concern ourselves, for example, with whether or not Pliable is going to make it. When we first meet him, his doom is written in the name Bunyan gives him. And yet, despite this, the narrative holds our attention. We know *that* Christian is going to make it, but how he is going to make it is the true mystery.

An allegory is a story with two "stories," stories of another sort. The first story, the ground floor, is the story of the characters or individuals involved. The second story is the floor of abstractions. Talkative on the ground floor is that particular character, occupying *that* particular place in the story. On the second story, he becomes all who share in those characteristics. On the second story, he is the abstraction of talkativeness.

Allegories lend themselves to stiffness, and when it comes to the allegorical part, *The Pilgrim's Progress* is no exception. But the thing that makes it come alive, and indeed to stand out from other allegories, is the *life* in the dialogue. As C.S. Lewis points out, Bunyan had almost perfect pitch when it came to recapturing the kind of conversation that would have occurred every day in the streets of Bedford.

The theology portrayed is Puritan theology, and of the stoutest sort. But we may make the additional observation that it is what we might call blue-collar Puritanism. Bunyan was a genius, but he was not formally educated or a university man. He was the kind of man schools are named after, not the kind of man who goes to them. If you ever read John Bunyan's spiritual autobiography, *Grace Abounding*, it will be brought home to you that conversion for Bunyan was "agonistic." There was a great deal of *wrestling* involved. This is the way it was for Bunyan himself, and this is the way it is for Christian, the protagonist in his great allegory.

So then, *The Pilgrim's Progress* is the story of Christian's conversion. Christian comes under conviction of sin. He lives in the City of Destruction and he knows for a fact that it is going to be destroyed. He knows that he himself is complicit in the crimes of his city—he has a great burden of sins on his back. These are not the sins of his nation or people—these are his *own* sins, his own contributions to the reason why the City of Destruction is under the wrath of God.

When Christian flees "from the wrath to come," he does so with his own burden on his back. He runs from the city where wrath was going to fall, but the trouble with his flight was that he took the occasion of wrath with him. It is bound tightly to his back, and as fast as he might run, his sin is always right behind him. This is the way it was for Bunyan also—this part of the story is plainly autobiographical. Bunyan broke with his old sinful and carefree life, and was bent on living differently . . . but his sins still went with him.

Although the burden of sins is carried on this pilgrimage for a time, it is a very short time, not a lifetime. The whole point of the pilgrimage is to come to a resolution—on *that* point at least. Early on in his journey, when he comes to the cross, Christian comes to the point of his decisive conversion. His pilgrimage was underway before that point, but this is where his pilgrimage *really* begins. Prior to the cross, his pilgrimage represents repentance. When he comes to the cross, he is converted (regeneration), and that represents faith. And this is the order we find in the New Testament—repent and believe.

Everything after the cross (regeneration/justification) is a matter of sanctification, which is the pathway to glorification. There may be great struggles and difficulties after that point of conversion, but they are different in kind from what went before. When Christian is shut up in Doubting Castle later on, for example, he does not *know* that he was saved. It is, after all, *Doubting* Castle. But earlier, when he was in the City of Destruction, he knew for a fact that he was *not* saved. At that point he had, you might say, assurance of damnation.

In other words, while he does not always have full and complete assurance of salvation during his time as a pilgrim, during the last portion of his unconverted years, before he came to the cross, he has true assurance that he was genuinely lost. Doubt is one thing and conviction of sin quite another. Once Christian has come to the cross, and the burden of his sins had been rolled away, Bunyan seeks to show us that assurance of salvation is the normal state of affairs. Christian doesn't always have it, but it is clear throughout the book that he is *supposed* to have it.

When he does not possess it, as when he gets off the path and winds up in Doubting Castle, it is clear that he is in these straits because he has disobeyed. The same thing is true when he misplaces his Roll. When he had been forgiven at the cross, one of the things he was given was a Roll, which he was to read along the way for encouragement, and which he was to present when he got to the Celestial City as his passport. But when he is ascending the Hill of Difficulty, he takes a break on the way up and while sleeping there loses his Roll. He notices it missing later, and goes back for it and finds it, but in the meantime, something has gone wrong. This is because the normal state of affairs is supposed to be assurance.

The book has resonated over centuries the way it has because Christian is very much Everyman, at least Everyman in the Church. The conflicts he has to deal with are conflicts that almost all readers have had to deal with as well. The obstacles he has to overcome are *common* obstacles. This means that the reader is summoned to stay interested because there is a sense in which he is reading his own autobiography. This holds his interest for two reasons. First, it is autobiographical and we always like reading about ourselves. Second, even though it is autobiographical, we didn't write it, and are consistently surprised by what comes next. We are surprised at the resemblance to our own lives, and we are surprised by the solutions or angles we had not thought of.

Another thing to notice is the content of the pilgrims' speech. They are quite *intentional* in their pilgrimage. The conversations they have along the way—whether with fellow pilgrims or with the hypocrites and flakes—show us pilgrims who listen to the sermons they hear, and who can reproduce the main point of those sermons in ordinary conversation. These are not conversations cast in sermonic form—these are conversations between ordinary people who listen intently to the sermons that they do hear. This is what ordinary conversation sounds like when theology is infused into it.

In one sense, the structure of the pilgrimage is quite simple. In another, it is astoundingly difficult. That is, it is simple to understand but very hard to do. The path is solitary, and the direction is defined. The task is to stay on the road. "Stay on the path, and go *that* way." The remarkable thing here is how hard it is to do such a simple thing. There are distractions and shortcuts, but the task assigned is simply to put one foot in front of the other on this one path. What is so hard about that?

When Christian and Faithful come to Vanity Fair, there is nothing complicated about the persecution presented to them. They do not conform to the ways of the town, and so they must be punished. This is very simple—B follows A, or, if you choose "wisely," D follows C. Death follows faithfulness, or, if you capitulate, pardon follows apostasy. This is not a world of nuance. A number of the characters (like Worldly Wiseman) might pretend nuance, but everything is really pretty straightforward. But we like to overthink it, and this is how we make a simple world complicated. Put another way, sin is what complicates reality, not actual sophistication.

Like the story of each of our lives, like the history of the world, like the promises of redemption down through Scripture, the plot of *The Pilgrim's Progress* is *linear*. The City of Destruction lies on one end, the Celestial City is on the other, and a road runs between them. The difficulties are all in the execution, not in the understanding. The way Christian escapes from Doubting Castle is by remembering that he had a key called Promise, and he had it in his possession the entire time. In a certain sense, the whole journey is like the Hill of Difficulty. There are lions at the gate of the Palace Beautiful, but they are chained. Apollyon really does stand in the way, but with the armor he has been given, Christian is able to fight him successfully.

One of the reasons why some people dislike allegory like this is because everything seems to them to be so screamingly obvious. The whole project seems like a ham-handed political cartoon from the 1950s, where all the characters are drawn with obvious lines, and all of them have tags sticking out of the back of their coat collars with things like "Capitalists" or "Corrupt Senators" written on the tags. It just seems so lame.

But the reason it seems lame to some is because they are not seriously on pilgrimage themselves. The difficulty in the pilgrimage is not usually in the understanding. If you read this book as entertainment, it might seem too obvious. Everything is laid out for you. All the characters are labeled. But if you *identify with* Christian and his struggles, as faithful readers do, the results are quite different. If you were told that if you did not deny Christ, the people who arrested you were going to pull your fingernails out one by one, the difficulty for you would not be lessened if the head kidnapper had a t-shirt that said Mr. Torturer on it. He would still have your interest.

A few words need to be said about the literary genius of John Bunyan. Most great books, once they are placed in the literary pantheon, are left to enjoy that place of honor. But Bunyan's presence in that cluster of literary worthies has been routinely resented.

One who did *not* resent it was C.S. Lewis. Indeed, Lewis understood Bunyan's gifts quite well: "We must attribute Bunyan's style to a perfect natural ear, a great sensibility for the idiom and cadence of popular speech, a long experience in addressing unlettered audiences, and a freedom from bad models."[6]

Bunyan lived in a time when "this means that" allegory was popular. It had been popular through the medieval period, and still held an honored position. Not only were literary allegories appreciated, but so was this kind of thinking. A genre called "emblem books" was very popular in Europe in the 16th and 17th centuries—these were detailed illustrations with allegorical meaning, accompanied by explanatory text. It was the kind of thing you could spend an evening poring over—instead of what enlightened people do now, which is watch HBO. The appreciation for emblem decoding can be seen in *The Pilgrim's Progress* at the House of the Interpreter. The general population had a real appetite for this kind of thing. We can hardly fault an author like Bunyan for writing to satisfy

---

6. C. S. Lewis, *Selected Literary Essays*, ed. Walter Hooper, 1st ed. (New York: HarperOne, 2013), 202.

that appetite, especially if he did it in a way that can only be described as marvelous.

To dismiss his achievement because a callow critic in the 21st-century once attended a weekend writer's workshop in which the form of allegory was sneered at, would be like disparaging the achievement of the first Renaissance painter to discover the central vanishing point because he failed to use acrylic paints, not invented until the 1940s.

One of reasons why people are so reluctant to give Bunyan the credit that is obviously due is because he was also, equally obviously, a Puritan. *The Pilgrim's Progress* is a work of explicit Puritan devotion. Puritan doctrines are woven throughout. The reason this is such a great problem is that one of the canards thrown at those who love the Puritans is that they are supposed to have no artistic soul. Puritans are supposed to be dour, solemn, and tight-lipped, possessing all the aesthetic sensibilities of a bowling ball.

If this is a central talking point about the Puritans, and it is, and we recognize the literary achievements of certain writers acknowledged as not being slouches—men like Bunyan, Herbert, Sidney, Defoe, Milton, Spenser, et al.—and then discover that all of them were of a Puritan cast, we might have to revisit our thesis. Shoot, we might have to surrender our thesis as a mere ungrounded slander, and kind of a wild one.

A much more reasonable hypothesis would be that different forms of religious devotion encourage the cultivation of different expressions of the aesthetic impulse that is present in all men, and as it happens, classical Protestantism is the natural home of *literary* arts—poems and stories and novels. It would be a refreshing thesis to advance, and it would have the exhilarating advantage of numerous exhibits that could be offered in defense of it. One of those exhibits, and a central one, would be *The Pilgrim's Progress.*

QUOTABLES

1. "What God says is best, is best, though all the men in the world are against it."

    ~ Faithful (p. 86)

2. "Now I saw in my dream, that the highway, up which Christian was to go, was fenced on either side with a wall, and that wall was called Salvation. Up this way, therefore, did burdened Christian run, but not without great difficulty, because of the load on his back. He ran thus till he came at a place somewhat ascending; and upon that place stood a cross, and a little below, in the bottom, a sepulchre. So I saw in my dream, that just as Christian came up with the cross, his burden loosed from off his shoulders, and fell from off his back, and began to tumble, and so continued to do till it came to the mouth of the sepulchre, where it fell in, and I saw it no more."

    ~ Narrator (p. 45)

3.   "Dark clouds bring waters, when the bright bring none."

~ Author's Apology (p. 3)

4.   "I have given Him my faith, and sworn my allegiance to Him; how, then, can I go back from this, and not be hanged as a traitor?"

~ Christian, to Apollyon (p. 67)"

5.   "He that lives in sin, and looks for happiness hereafter, is like him that soweth cockle and thinks to fill his barn with wheat or barley."

~ The Interpreter, in Part the Second

6.   "A man there was, / though some did count him mad, / the more he cast away / the more he had."

~ Honest, in Part the Second.

21 SIGNIFICANT QUESTIONS AND ANSWERS

1. What is the significance of the first line of the book: "as I walked through the wilderness of this world, I lighted on a certain place where was a den, and laid me down to sleep, and as I slept I dreamed a dream."

   Bunyan was in jail (or as the English spell it, gaol) when he wrote much of this book, and so it is not surprising that he had the dream in a "den." And Bunyan takes a passing image of a pilgrimage in this world from Scripture, and develops it brilliantly. "Dearly beloved, I beseech you as *strangers and pilgrims*, abstain from fleshly lusts, which war against the soul; Having your conversation honest among the Gentiles: that, whereas they speak against you as evildoers, they may by your good works, which they shall behold, glorify God in the day of visitation" (1 Peter 2:11–12 KJV). This world is not a place for settling down—it is described by

Bunyan as a wilderness—and so there is a need for pilgrimage through this world, and then over the river and clean out of it. Remember also that when the children of Israel were in the wilderness, they were a nomadic people—pilgrims.

2. What is the overall structure of the world in *The Pilgrim's Progress*?

There is the City of Destruction on one end, and the Celestial City on the other. A road with many dangers runs between the two cities, and in order to get to the Celestial City, a final river must be crossed. In between are many distractions, obstacles, and enemies, but also some encouragements and friends.

3. Speaking of obstacles and distractions, what does the village of Morality represent? What about Mr. Legality and his son Civility?

In Bunyan's day, he would have been thinking about the formal superficiality of Roman Catholicism and the Church of England—although Catholicism in 1678 would not have been the force in England it once had been. But the picture Bunyan draws is certainly still applicable today to all sorts of people who just want to be "moral people." In other words, the "establishment" church is the respectable church, and those who always want to "do what's done" will figure out a way to go to that church. As circumstances and conditions vary, the name of the religious establishment will also vary. And as time goes on, some people who are more secular in temperament will figure out a way to have a village called Morality with no formal worship whatever. But in any case, the focus is on manners and externals, as opposed to sincerity of heart.

4.   Who are some of the characters that reflect some problems with the Church of England?

The overall problem is formalism in religion, people just checking off boxes. In this book some examples of this kind of superficial faith would include Mr. Worldly Wiseman, Formalist and Hypocrisy, Talkative, and Ignorance.

We can see how deeply committed to a superficial religion some people are by what they are willing to do to defend it. Remember that Bunyan wrote this book in jail, placed there by *Christian* magistrates. We may forgive him if he took a dim view of their spiritual health. In this book, some examples of persecution of Bunyan's style of non-conformity would be the treatment of Christian and Faithful in Vanity Fair, as well as the symbol of the lions. Lions symbolize persecution for obvious reasons, going back to the early church.

5.   What does Mount Sinai represent?

When God first appeared to Israel on Mount Sinai, He was the one who had just delivered them from the bondage of slavery in Egypt. He says as much in the preamble to the Ten Commandments. But

by the time of Paul's letter to the Galatians, Mount
Sinai had come to represent slavery—coming to
Mount Sinai the wrong way meant going into
slavery. When the Reformers emphasized law and
grace, law and gospel, they were considering this
reality. Yes, the Old Testament law had been twisted
into something it shouldn't have been, but by the
time of the apostles it had taken on enough of a
life of its own to be called a "covenant with Hagar."
And so for Bunyan, Mount Sinai represents condemnation. It is quite striking reversal of symbols—
Sinai began as a symbol of liberation from Egypt
and gradually became a symbol of renewed slavery
in Egypt.

6. What must Christian do?

> He must get away from the City of Destruction,
> and he must get rid of the burden that is on his
> back.

7. What was conversion like for Bunyan? And once a
    man was converted, what was the ordinary assumption
    about assurance? Before Christian fled from the City of
    Destruction, what did he have assurance of?

> Bunyan thought of conversion in "agonistic" terms.
> The ordinary course of affairs for Bunyan was that a
> converted man ought to have assurance of salvation.
> If he did not, then something out of the ordinary
> had occurred, like being trapped in Doubting
> Castle. Before he fled from his hometown, he had

an assurance of damnation or condemnation.

Christian is directed first to the Wicket Gate, who is Christ. A wicket gate is a narrow, small gate, which is what Christ is for us. So Christian is saved there, but does not experience liberation or assurance of that salvation until he comes to the cross and his burden falls off.

8. Some people criticize Bunyan for individualism, seeing the Christian life as being all about getting to heaven rather than about doing good works on earth. What about the *church*? What about sharing the gospel with others, as we see in the New Testament?

The first thing to keep in mind is that an allegory cannot do everything. Isolating one particular aspect of the Christian life and then demanding that emphasis from somebody who was doing something else entirely is more than a little unfair. In the second place, there is a place for manuals of personal devotion since we can control our own behavior. This helps us prioritize our own conduct, which is what we are actually responsible for. And last, Bunyan does add a community of pilgrims in Part 2, which is full of examples clearly culled from his pastoral experience. And even in Part 1, Christian is accompanied, first by Faithful and then by Hopeful. While the emphasis is on individual salvation, this book never promotes a solitary pilgrimage.

9. Some people think that Ignorance goes to hell for not getting arcane theological distinctions straight. Is Bunyan being not very charitable here?

> The main problem with Ignorance is not what he does not know. His problem is what he is not willing to know. He does not repent in the least, and his behavior is markedly willful. He is not teachable. In other words, we see immediately that he is ignorant for a reason. It is not Bunyan being uncharitable with Ignorance, but rather moderns being uncharitable with Bunyan. The "justification" language used by Christian is hardly "technical," and the fact that we identify with Ignorance so readily might mean that we are identifying with his condition rather than his plight. Shallow and "propositionless" faith is still a very real problem today.

10. Apart from Doubting Castle, what was another occasion when Christian lost his assurance? What are some examples of characters or situations that clearly came out of Bunyan's melancholy and long struggle with assurance?

> When he lost the Roll that had been given to him. He took a rest on the Hill of Difficulty, and lost it while he was sleeping. That Roll was his passport to the Celestial City.
>
> With regard to melancholy in general, we would have to consider the burden on Christian's back, the Slough of Despond, the battle with Apollyon, the

Valley of the Shadow of Death, Giant Despair and his castle, and the River of Death. Think of Luther's fits of melancholy interpreted as demonic. We tend to think of these things in terms of chemical imbalances, while our fathers in the faith saw them as parts of a great spiritual war. In many ways they were closer to the truth, and their images have proven more helpful to more people over the years than our pills have.

11. What are some of the reasons for the perennial appeal of *The Pilgrim's Progress*?

Bunyan is writing about Everyman, or at least Everyman in the Church. All of the struggles and trials are relevant to us. We like it because it is in some measure autobiographical. Another reason is that it is written well. The conversations and dialog are very much like real conversations.

12. Are the choices that are presented to the pilgrims sophisticated or nuanced?

No, not really. Their task is simple: stay on the path. The obstacles are frequently just as simple—either telling them to stop, as Apollyon, or distracting them off the path, which is how they wind up in Doubting Castle.

13. Why do some people dislike allegory? Why do modern readers who are serious Christians not trip over the allegorical element as much?

Because it seems too obvious to them, and they
want more nuance. It seems unsophisticated, and
unlike anything one of the cool kids would have
written. Serious Christians don't struggle with this
as much because they identify with Christian and
his struggles, and the difficulty of the pilgrimage is
not usually a difficulty of understanding. It is the
difficulty of doing.

14. What was an emblem book?

It was a book of illustrations with allegorical meaning, and with explanatory text accompanying it. It
is the kind of thing that Christian experienced in
the House of the Interpreter. This kind of thing was
very popular, and a delight to multiple generations.
When we disparage this kind of thing we are only
demonstrating how culturally parochial we are.

15. Why does the modern unpopularity of allegory reflect
on Bunyan? How is this criticism anachronistic? How is
this unfair to artists of previous eras?

Because we disparage the form itself, we have come
to believe that great artistic achievement within
that form is not possible. The criticism is anachronistic because it fails to recognize the different
circumstances that other artists were dealing with,
and expects them to conform to our limitations. It
is unfair to previous eras because it expects them to
have access to things that were not yet invented or
developed. Indeed it expects them to have access to

inventions that were actually dependent upon their
initial contributions.

16. What is different about Bunyan when it comes to his
presence among literary greats?

> Many people think of him as some sort of lucky
> intruder. They believe that he does not really belong
> in the Hall of Fame for writers. His presence there
> is begrudged.

17. What is frequently said about the aesthetic contributions of the Puritans as a class? Were there some
classical Protestant figures who were great writers or
poets? What would be an important exhibit if we were
seeking to show that classical Protestantism creates
an environment that is conducive to the production of
great literature?

> It is commonly claimed that the Protestants were
> aesthetically soulless. But against this groundless
> claim we may set men like Bunyan, Marvell, Sidney,
> Herbert, Donne, Taylor, Defoe, Milton, Spenser,
> and many more. One of our central exhibits would
> be found in *The Pilgrim's Progress*. We would point
> to the greatness of the work, alongside the lack of
> formal education on the part of the author.

18. Who was one great modern literary critic who appreciated the contribution of Bunyan?

> C.S. Lewis.

19. Where did Bunyan write much of *The Pilgrim's Progress*?

> He wrote much of it while in prison. He was there
> because he insisted on his right to preach without
> authorization from the state.

20. Was Bunyan narrow-minded, thinking that only people
    like him—and very few of them at that—could get into
    heaven?

> C.S. Lewis points out critics have never been
> imprisoned by the authorities. They should talk. In
> other words, when we talk about narrow-minded
> views, our first thoughts ought not to land on the
> guy in jail who is there for his opinions. That said,
> we have to remember that just because unbelieving
> cultures persecute Christians does not stop a lot of
> people from getting saved.

21. Why does Giant Despair not handle the sunlight well?

> One self-confessed melancholic said this: "If I had
> a superpower it would be finding the negative spin
> on any situation, and my skills seem to be especially
> acute after ten o'clock at night."[7] Those with dark
> thoughts gravitate to the darkness, and a bright
> sunny day with fluffy clouds is not really welcome.

---

7. Lindsey Tollefson, *The Psalms For Us* (Moscow, ID: Canon Press, 2017).

FURTHER DISCUSSION
AND REVIEW

Master what you have read by reviewing and integrating the different elements of this classic.

SETTING AND CHARACTERS

Be able to compare and contrast the personalities (including strengths, weaknesses, and mannerisms) of each character. Which characters change and which do not?

PLOT

Be able to describe the beginning, middle, and end of the book along with specific details that move the plot forward and make it compelling.

CONFLICT

Go through the character list and describe the tension between any and all main characters. What characters represent internal conflict within the Christian's life? What characters represent external situations or forces?

THEME STATEMENTS

Be able to describe what this classic is telling us about the world. Is the message true? What truth can we take from the plot, characters, conflict, and themes (even if the author didn't believe that truth)? Do any objects take on added meaning because of repetition or their place in the story (i.e., do any objects become symbols)? How does the author use perspective, tone, and irony to tell the truth?

- Being a Christian is often not about complex and nuanced moral decisions, but about the constant fight against sin.
- Salvation cannot be achieved through our own efforts, and true religion involves the heart, not just external worship and works.
- Write your own allegory: if John Bunyan were writing this great work today, do you think that there would be any new dangers that he would place along the road? What obstacles do you think he would leave out, if any, and what obstacles, do you think he would add?

A NOTE FROM THE PUBLISHER:
TAKING THE CLASSICS QUIZ

Once you have finished the worldview guide, you can prepare for the end-of-book test. Each test will consist of a short-answer section on the book itself and the author, a short-answer section on plot and the narrative, and a long-answer essay section on worldview, conflict, and themes.

Each quiz, along with other helps, can be downloaded for free at www.canonpress.com/ClassicsQuizzes. If you have any questions about the quiz or its answers or the Worldview Guides in general, you can contact Canon Press at service@canonpress.com or 208.892.8074.

ABOUT THE AUTHOR

Douglas Wilson has been a pastor of Christ Church in Moscow, Idaho for forty years. He has started both a K-12 Christian school and an accredited Christian college, and has written more than fifty books. He and his wife Nancy have three children (all of whom have written books of their own) and a bunch of grandchildren.

www.ingramcontent.com/pod-product-compliance
Lightning Source LLC
Chambersburg PA
CBHW071937020426
42331CB00010B/2916